Conversations
with Dogs

Conversations with Dogs

A Psychic Reveals
What Our Canine Companions
Have to Say
(and How You can Talk to Them, Too!)

By William Stillman

Published by Haunted Road Media, LLC
www.hauntedroadmedia.com

ISBN-13: 978-0998164953

DEDICATION

*For Alex, who became
a believer*

CONTENTS

PREFACE

"His name's Obie," said the dog's owner as I knelt to stroke the likeable yellow Lab. "He's so sweet and affectionate," I said as Obie rubbed up against me and burrowed his nose into my T-shirt. This scenario had become commonplace: Me, out for my once- or twice-daily neighborhood walk, happening upon a dog-walker, and being drawn to interact with their respective pups. "I can talk to dogs, you know," I offered.

"Really!" said Obie's owner, who later told me her name was Celeste. "That's so interesting. What is Obie saying about me?" Celeste wondered.

Once I relaxed my thoughts and focused a bit, I tried to "see" what it was that Obie *was* saying. In my mind's eye, I got the impression of a body of water and I felt a sense of longing. "He misses being in or near a pond or a pool of water," I ventured.

"Ohhhh," Celeste responded. "We recently moved here and he used to love the pool at the dog park I took him to. What else?"

I refocused and waited for more to be "impressed" within me. "I'm seeing that he should avoid eating or getting into hamburger, it could cause problems for him."

"That's funny!" said Celeste. "At our Fourth of July party, he *did* get up on a countertop and ate some hamburger that had been left sitting out. He got sick afterwards."

"What about Dillon?" asked Celeste, nodding toward Obie's older black Lab companion, tethered on a separate leash.

"I'm not getting anything from him, I'm afraid," I said, but in that moment Dillon, who had been lying quietly on the cement sidewalk, got up and teetered toward me. A moment later, the mind-pictures manifested. "He's passing the torch. He's aware that he's aging and he's making efforts to mentor Obie, when Obie's not distracted, that is," I interpreted, as Obie butted in between us and then sniffed absent-mindedly at the grass, as if to illustrate my point.

Celeste solemnly acknowledged that, indeed, Dillon was nearing the end of his life. I assuaged her anxiety by revealing that animals don't think in terms of life and death. They think in terms of a continuous cycle of energy that assumes different forms. (After this encounter, Celeste told me what a comforting thought that was and how it helped put Dillon's deteriorating health into perspective.)

"One last thing," I said, rising up from kneeling beside Dillon. "He just told me there's a baby coming."

"Oh, that must be about the horses we keep," said Celeste.

"No, no," I countered, "he means a human baby." Celeste conceded that her daughter had been married for three years but she and her husband hadn't had any luck conceiving. "Dillon suggests that she needs to *relax*," I told her. "Relax *here*," I emphasized as I pointed to my head. "Once she relaxes her  thoughts, the rest will come." I parted ways with Celeste and her dogs, and she expressed her great appreciation for the insight. In fact, she said, she was going to be speaking to her daughter once they got in from their walk, and she intended to share the information.

"What will you tell her?" I asked incredulously, "That a psychic said your dog told him if she chills out, she'll finally get pregnant?" We both had a chuckle about that, but in reality I wondered just how many people would've been as receptive as Celeste. In fact, if anyone had told me ten or fifteen years ago that I'd be talking to dogs, I would've said they were nuts! As it turns out, I'm not the only one capable of such a canine connection. If you'll read on, I'll tell you what I know—or rather what the dogs have told me.

INTRODUCTION

Dogs are a lot like people. Some are nice, and some are not so nice. Some are loaded with personality and good humor, while others are shy and reserved. Some dogs are self-absorbed and full of attitude; others possess a sense of duty and altruism. You don't need to be a psychic to appreciate the foregoing—those of us who are pet owners know that our dogs' personalities are usually unique to each pedigree, each breed, and each pooch. But what you may not know is that dogs have a lot to say beyond eat, drink, sniff, play, protect, and so on. Many dog owners can attest that they have a smart dog, though they may be surprised to learn just *how* smart. In other words, when when it comes to the average canine there's more than what meets the eye. According to a 2011 poll con-

ducted by the Associated Press and Petside.com, two thirds of American pet owners believe their animal companions have a sixth sense that alerts them to future events, such as severe weather or earthquakes, or gives them insight into their owners' lives.

There are many kinds of intelligence, and, by traditional standards, animals have smarts measurable well below that of human beings, *but* they are possessed of *emotional* intelligence that is on par with highly sensitive people. For example, while we all know that dogs have supersonic smelling capabilities and such keen acoustics they can hear sound frequencies the human ear cannot, dogs are also *empaths* meaning they are finely attuned to our moods. How many of us can tell of the times that our dogs shared in our excitement and happiness, or somehow knew exactly how to soothe us when we were sick or having a bad day?

Dogs are not only a reflection of who we are, they are *projections* of who we are. We've all heard that dogs look like their owners (and vice-versa), but dogs also resemble our general temperament.

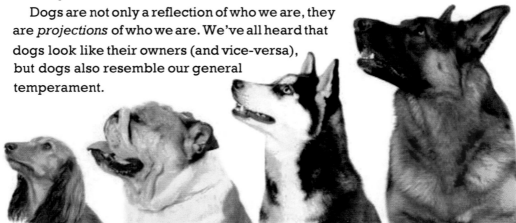

This book is a collection of interactions I've had with those emotionally-attuned dogs who allowed me the privilege of conversing with them. It is an intimate process and one I haven't always been able to engage in with *all* dogs—just those that deem me worthy. But, by and large, most dogs are ready to talk, to compliment and complain, and to spill the beans on their owners.

Not only will I share these dialogues, I'll tell how it works, and how you, too, can enjoy such opportunities for keener insights and a closer relationship with your beloved Fido, Fifi, or Rex.

Chapter One

ABOUT ME

I must tell you, this business of talking with dogs all began by happenstance. In fact, my first encounter communicating with a living creature wasn't with a dog at all; it was with a Praying Mantis! It was a lovely spring day, and I had the intention of spending time in my backyard. As I came out of my enclosed porch, I noticed a large Praying Mantis trying to climb up the vinyl siding of the porch. It wasn't having much success, as the siding wasn't offering any traction for the insect's struggling feelers. Desiring to be of assistance, I spied a nearby twig and, holding one end, extended it to the Mantis in an offer to help. I was a bit surprised and pleased that the Mantis immediately accepted the twig as the better alternative, and I quickly carried it to an overgrown hillside where I gently set both the twig and insect down. In a regal manner fitting so stately a creature, the Mantis disembarked and started making its way through the underbrush.

As I looked on in admiration, I was suddenly struck by an unexpected scene: The Mantis had deftly seized hold of a passing beetle and was cracking its shell like a walnut before consuming the beetle alive. (If you never know where your next meal's coming from, you take it where you can get it, I guess.) I was trying to reconcile the contrast between the Mantis' serene appearance and its cannibalism when, after it finished eating—I swear—the Mantis pivoted its head and stared directly at me, and in that moment, I was impressed with the thought, "Would you have me eat something already dead?" It was a sobering reality check—when I thought 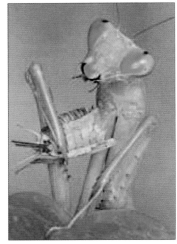 about it, no, I suppose I wouldn't expect a Praying Mantis to eat something already dead. Not that I had ever given it thought before, but it made sense when I considered how very few creatures are carcass scavengers. And while I can't say with absolute certainty that the communication came directly from the Mantis, it did ring true.

You might be thinking, "What an intriguing childhood memory," except that the incident with the Praying Mantis occurred in 2007 and I was in my forties! (In other words, I wasn't born knowing how to talk to dogs, and if I figured out how to do it later in life, so can you!)

I was an unusual child, quiet and introverted. I spent *a lot* of time alone. even though I was the oldest of four boys, I could not relate well with my peers. I was not socially involved and outgoing like my brothers. Instead, I spent the majority of my free time in my bedroom drawing, reading, or creating projects I'd dream up. So disconnected was I, that my brothers played with neighborhood children who didn't even realize they *had* an older brother, because I was virtually invisible.

Words that others used to describe me included weird, antisocial, moody and irritable, hypersensitive, cold, arrogant and aloof, and gifted. The words that would've better summed it up—as I know now—are Asperger's Syndrome, a mild, high-functioning experience on the autism spectrum marked by average to above-average intelligence, sensory sensitivities (like aversion to noise and bright light), intense focus on topics of special interest and the aforementioned social challenges. For being so different, I endured years of bullying at the hands of schoolmates which ultimately left me traumatized, depressed, and, at one point, suicidal.

I was a product of my environment, however, and I see my own peculiar traits in other family members. As emotionally detached as we were, though, I am glad for two things. First, my parents were animal lovers, particularly my mother, who was always one to rescue abandoned baby birds and wayward bunnies. Growing up we had just about every conceivable creature as pets, from dogs and cats to ducks, gerbils, Guinea pigs, mice, hamsters, fish and rabbits. (Once, I almost got a de-scented skunk as a birthday present, but my mother wasn't quite satisfied with its temperament.)

Second, my family was always open to discussing the plausibility of the unexplained. Not once was anything seemingly improbable to others ever dismissed as nonsense, and topics such as UFOs, Bigfoot and ghosts could be openly discussed at the dinner table with the qualification that humankind can't possibly have all the answers, and some things will always remain a mystery.

I don't recall feeling a strong emotional attachment to any of our pets in particular, which might strike readers as odd; but then, I wasn't in a position to emotionally reciprocate much of anything. Being in survival mode, I was selfish and self-centered. I wasn't unkind to animals but I was often indifferent, which I now regret as we had some very loyal dogs that deserved better than to be taken for granted.

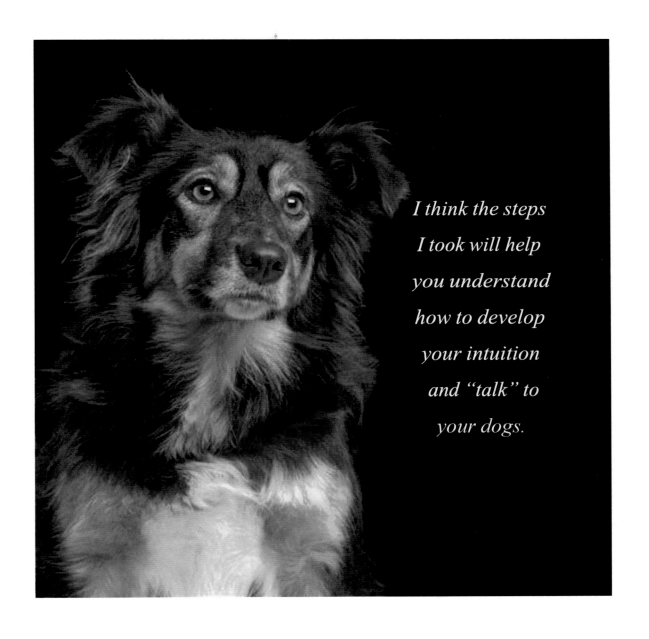

*I think the steps
I took will help
you understand
how to develop
your intuition
and "talk" to
your dogs.*

I have previously written about my personal pathway to self-reflection and discovery in a few of my autism books, and I suppose (and hope!) that each of us comes to make peace with ourselves in our own way, in our own time. For me, the journey combined all that I am into a clear trajectory: Take the truth of my faults, flaws and frailties, and *apply it* in order to be of service to others. And of this process was born the ability to better connect not just with people but animals as well. I think the steps I took will help you understand how to develop your intuition and "talk" to your dogs. But more about this later.

A major portion of my path was to work with children, teens, and adults who are on the autism spectrum. They are my people. And the more I found a communion with these folks and their families, the more my own sensitivities reawakened in such a way that I could provide them with guidance and consultation *intuitively*, which was accurate about 90 percent of the time.

This came through most profoundly in my ability to "read" photographs of individuals with autism given only their first name and age, and no prior information. Through this method, I could provide parents with insights and impressions about their loved one that they may have misinterpreted as something contradictory. For example, the child who appeared behaviorally hyperactive was, in reality, distraught about his father's recent incarceration—only thing is, no one thought to tell him because they didn't think he'd understand!

What I found, however, was that occasionally when making autism consultations on home visits, various family dogs would be attracted to me, and I would get what I came to call "bleed-over." That is, while I was present for the purpose of assessing the family dynamics, oftentimes a dog would want my attention more than what is typical, and would stare deeply into my eyes.

Once, as if to make a statement, a German Shepherd parked himself directly in front of me and placed his paw in my lap; as it happened, there was a lot of stress and tension in the household that required dissecting through intensive discussion — the Shepherd wanted to make sure I got it. After this happened, the dog and slept at my feet. On another occasion, a Bassett Hound would not leave me alone despite his owner persisting in calling him away. I finally understood: This dog had something to say! So I interjected, "No, no, it's okay, he has something to tell me." And here's what the dog told me: It turns out his stomach was bothering him (an ongoing issue for which he had taken medication in the past) and he wanted some chicken broth to soothe it! The family had previously given the dog chicken broth and, after I left, the owner ran out and bought some more. I was told that, afterward, the dog seemed to feel better and sat by the front door awaiting my return.

I thought this sort of thing was only possible so long as I was "in the zone" for my autism consultations. However, during one of my excursions, I was enjoying some "off-duty" downtime in the living room of a professional colleague. I began to get impressions from her older dog. Specifically, the dog felt embarrassed and wanted to apologize for a couple of recent accidents on the carpet, which couldn't be helped. My colleague confirmed that, indeed, there had been several such incidents and the emotion of shame communicated by the dog gave my friend a greater sense of compassion for her pet's situation.

"Interesting," I thought. Talking with dogs can happen independently of my consulting work! Still, I chalked it up to a curiosity and didn't think much of it. That is until one eventful afternoon that would change everything.

Chapter Two

A Motley Crew

Anyone who has lost their voice for more than a couple days will tell you that well-intentioned people begin second guessing their wants and needs; but the majority of the time, those same people completely misunderstand and misinterpret the desired wants and needs. Like the person who's lost their voice, dog behavior is frequently misconstrued as well. For example, the dog who barks incessantly when the doorbell rings may be perceived as a nuisance when, in actuality, the dog believes she *has* to bark loudly because her owners don't hear the bell!

It was this premise of misperception that prompted my aunt to openly wonder what her four dogs were thinking and why, it seemed, they were prone to assorted misbehaviors. Now, before delving into what transpired I must tell you something that makes the circumstances all the more remarkable. I have a lot of obsessive-compulsive peculiarities and I like to keep my hands clean. Three of my aunt's dogs are large and loud and shed quite a bit, so I never really paid much attention to them. I kept my distance and—after not getting attention from me—they kept theirs. (I wasn't even certain of their names to be honest. That's how little I acknowledged them.)

But one weekend afternoon in spring 2010 when I was visiting, my aunt and her husband were discussing the challenges each of the dogs presented behaviorally. (Three were rescue dogs from a kennel that specialized in Golden Retrievers, and all came with their individual anxieties and eccentricities—just like people.) We had finished a lunch my aunt prepared and were unwinding in their sun porch. The dogs were there, of course, and in this relaxed state I began to think, or rather *feel*, that I could tap into the personality of each. It was all rather spontaneous and I wasn't sure of the validity for any of what I was sharing. To my surprise, my aunt and her husband not only validated what came spilling forth, they later told me it completely altered their perspective as pet owners!

First was Morgan, a male Golden Retriever. Morgan was lying near me but when I began to tune into him, he actually got up and sat next to me. In my mind, I saw a five-star officer's badge, and I told everyone, "Morgan's the chief of police. He takes his role as protector very seriously, and he would appreciate it if that were recognized. His job is to maintain order in the household and he is not above nipping at the others to make it so." Not only did my aunt verify what I had just stated, Morgan reacted, too. As I espoused his contributions, his posture

straightened and his chest swelled with pride! Morgan was definitely an alpha-male and dominated the other dogs.

He also "said" that another dog was coming, to which everyone had a good chuckle, and my aunt denied that a fifth dog was even conceivable. (What I didn't say at the time was that Morgan didn't mean an addition. He meant a *replacement*. I didn't clarify the communication further for fear of causing undue upset—not to mention I could always be wrong.)

Next was Jonah, a female Golden Retriever. (Jonah was originally thought to be a male, hence her name. By the time it was realized she was indeed of the female gender, the name had already stuck.) Jonah "told" me that she is very, very sensitive. This extends to her hearing, her teeth, and her gastrointestinal system. But most of all, she didn't like storms. My aunt confirmed this and said that during a storm, Jonah will hide in the bathroom and wait it out. My aunt said that when she opens up the backdoor for everyone to go outside, Jonah nips at the others' hindquarters as they exit. The reason, as Jonah told it, was that she had a fear that they would leave and not come back. This was precipitated by a frustrating spree of escapes, led by Morgan from the backyard which was fenced in, booby-trapped, and otherwise barricaded in increasingly intricate ways. But like Houdini, Morgan always found a way to outsmart and outwit the ante as it was raised. Jonah must've known what Morgan was plotting, and, by nipping at his heels, was chastising him for it.

The third dog was Orson, my aunt's Saint Bernard, a big, mushy baby of a dog who didn't seem terribly bright and craved

constant attention—the kind of dog that, if you stopped petting him because you thought he was asleep or relaxed, he'd instantly revive and beg for more. Indeed, Orson (whom I had often mistakenly called Seymour!) explained that he had been taken from his mother too early, and this accounted for his continuous need to be stroked and cuddled, even though his size made it sometimes awkward or even uncomfortable to share space with him. (Jonah had referred to Orson as "the other one" and indicated that she found him uncouth and lacking in good manners.)

Another problem Orson posed was that at mealtimes he would park himself next to my aunt and persistently place his paw in her lap, even though he knew the routine was he'd be fed following dinner. As I continued an internal dialogue with Orson, the impression I received was, "If you've ever been without food, you would understand." I interpreted this to mean that, wherever it was that Orson came from originally, there were occasions when food was scarce or he didn't get enough to eat. To quell this anxiety, I instructed my aunt to give him a little something to eat *before* the meal as this might stop what was perceived as nuisance begging. The next time I came over for lunch, we tried it. Sure enough, Orson laid down near us and allowed us to eat uninterrupted.

Finally, there was Rusty, a Sheltie and Pomeranian mix that had been my grandmother's dog. (My aunt inherited Rusty when my grandmother became increasingly elderly and frail, and required nursing home

care.) As was true of the other dogs, little was known of Rusty's background, except that he had led a very isolated existence, kept in a kennel with little to no interaction with people or other dogs. When my grandmother had him, he spent the entire day in a little bed next to hers, leaving only to eat and go outside. He would not go for walks, nor would he greet visitors. (I always had a soft spot for Rusty because he struck me as a doggie equivalent to someone with autism.) Since coming to live with my aunt and her husband, Rusty slowly became a bit more social, and he was quite the watchdog, barking ten minutes in advance of anyone arriving at the door.

As I was tapping into Rusty, he actually came out and positioned himself two rooms away but clearly within my view, as if he were listening intently to make sure I got it right. What I got from Rusty was that he is highly intelligent and not of this world! He is here to learn compromise, which is challenging. While the other dogs are focused on sounds, smells, and the household pecking order, he was concerned with intellectual thinking (and as such can't relate to them). As I shared these impressions, Rusty stared at me intently and sat very still. But the moment I concluded speaking about him, he stood up and left the room, retreating to his spot in my aunt's bedroom once again.

A couple weeks after this visit, my aunt informed me that Morgan, the police chief, had been diagnosed with lymphoma. Tumors were growing rapidly around his throat. Rather than subject him to radiation treatments, my aunt determined to keep him as comfortable as possible. Prednisone helped keep the tumors in check but made Morgan exceedingly thirsty. On my next visit, my aunt asked if I could ask Morgan how he was feeling. He happened to be lying near me, and I tried connecting with him. The first impression I got was also the most poignant: He showed me a setting sun, slowly fading in resonance like a burning ember against a purple sky. He accepted his fate calmly and felt only some pressure—not pain—around his throat. (On occasions following this, he would come up to me and deliberately place his throat in my open palm.) As I finished sharing this vision with my aunt, Morgan sat up and offered me his paw—everyone was awed. It was so unusual. I had never seen him do this before. It was as if to say, "Thank you for being my interpreter." A matter of months later, Morgan's tumors had doubled in size. He had no desire to eat or drink, so my aunt made the decision to have him euthanized—his life had run its course. He must've known it too—remember, well before being diagnosed, he predicted that he would be replaced. What he couldn't foretell was that the chief of police could only be retired, not replaced.

Chapter Three

Dog Tales

As was true of conversing with Morgan, Jonah, Orson, and Rusty, my experiences talking with other dogs were by chance and usually occurred during my daily afternoon or evening walks. My neighborhood is part of a vast development sandwiched between two other heavily populated complexes of townhouses and single-family houses. My neighborhood connects with another complex at the back by sharing a common street and a walking path, which runs between both developments. I say this because most of the dogs I meet while out walking are dogs I've never seen before, have met only once, and have never seen again, or at least not for many long months at a time.

In this chapter, I'll profile, journal-style, just a few of the many dogs I've met, and will reveal what it is they've had to say. And because I'm human and never one-hundred percent accurate, I'm including the misses as well as the hits. As you're reading, bear in mind that the dog owners were present and, for the most part, able to validate what I was telling them.

Name: Daisy
Breed: Lhasa Apso

Daisy belongs to a former neighbor, so before she moved away, I got to see her often. She craved affection and licked my face a lot. Early on in our relationship, she would get so excited to see me, she'd spontaneously pee! (It's a good thing I don't have that effect on everyone!) Daisy always made me laugh because her head looked just like a daisy in full bloom. Daisy has a tough assignment: Her "mom" grapples with clinical depression and her "dad" is an alcoholic. There's a lot of heated arguing in their household, which I have overheard on a couple occasions walking past their home. Suffice it to say, Daisy's job is to bring cheer and lightheartedness to her immediate atmosphere, which is easier said than done. I think Daisy is stronger than she looks, for which I am glad; she needs to be.

Names: Midge and Butch

Breeds: Pekingese and Boxer

Midge and Butch both moved away but I always enjoyed meeting up with them. Despite the difference in their size, Midge gave the orders; she definitely projected an attitude of superiority and entitlement. She had a certain place to rest that was hers alone (and she had no qualm about making that known should the occasion arise). She also was susceptible to

cigarette smoke (the owner's husband was a smoker, as I learned). Butch didn't have much to say except that he was content with his subservient role and accepted his task of obedience.

Name: Scruffy

Breed: Terrier mix

Scruffy was being walked by a married couple. He is very small and typically shies away from strangers but warmed up to me such that now when I see him, he comes running to greet me. He has a tendency to get into things on walks, and his owners should check between the pads on his paws for bits of gravel and twigs. He also likes the man's daughter (who Scruffy was missing because she was away). His role is to amuse and entertain, and he very much lives up to it—he is such a funny, silly little thing!

Name: Zhu Zhu

Breed: Pekingese

As I was approaching, Zhu Zhu started yapping at me and gave off lots of attitude as if I was being intrusive of her turf. (Zhu Zhu very much projected a little princess-type affect.) Once I knelt down and spoke in a soothing tone, Zhu Zhu became a bit more tolerant. She said she liked the taste of chicken, and had a favorite spot to sit in at home—a spot no one else better commandeer or they'd be subjected to the wrath of Zhu Zhu! She was, though, afraid of storms, and had a delicate respiratory system such that she can't tolerate cigarette smoke. She also thought of her owner more like a sister than a mother. (The young woman shared that Zhu

Zhu "calls" her mother "mom.") The longer I represented Zhu Zhu authentically, the more Zhu Zhu calmed and eventually dropped the attitude altogether. Before parting ways, Zhu Zhu even allowed me to pet her!

Name: Dante

Breed: German Shepherd

Dante was largely preoccupied with sights and scents but told me that he liked going to a pond where he could chase the ducks. He was also bothered by storms but didn't show it outwardly as he wanted to live up to his owner's rather macho expectations.

Names: Unknown

Breed: Chihuahua

Two Chihuahuas who would not stop barking at me, wouldn't settle, and wouldn't come near without showing their teeth. No matter how hard I tried to be still and gentle, they just weren't having it. A wash-out.

Names: Mabel and Sweetie

Breed: Greyhounds

Early one evening, a couple was walking two greyhounds and as I approached, one (named Mabel) stopped in her tracks and wouldn't budge. I knelt down and told the wife that Mabel was very sensitive and had a very sensitive stomach. Mabel was homesick and missed being able to run freely. She was also feeling stress and pressure in her hind quarters and hip area, and to please be patient with her if she was having trouble keeping up. The wife told me that Mabel is, indeed, very sensitive with stomach issues. They had *just* moved to our development. Previously, they had been able to just open up the backdoor and let both dogs run. The husband told me that Mabel has a degenerative muscular disease affecting her hind quarters and hips. In a lovely and compassionate touch, the woman apologized to Mabel for not understanding. After interpreting for Mabel, she became very affectionate and rested her head against mine. (Oddly, a little way further on my walk, a feral cat I had seen the night before came over and rubbed itself against me!)

Sweetie is Mabel's cohabitant. Sweetie didn't have a lot to say but wanted to be recognized for her intelligence, which she indicated was greater than Mabel's! She had an uncanny knack for problem-solving in order to get what she wanted. By comparison, the owner thought Mabel was merely being patient. She also likes when children come to visit, which they do.

Names: Faith and Duke

Breed: Boxers

These dogs belong to the adult daughter of a neighbor who has since moved out

of town but was visiting her folks. I happened upon them beyond my neighborhood on the walking path. I had met Faith previously but not Duke. My neighbor said Duke was skittish with men, but once I kneeled down, Duke sniffed me and licked my face, which surprised my neighbor. Duke was guarded about revealing much, other than that he had an abusive background. He was really trying to do his best and meet expectations, but he wished the man of the house (my neighbor's new husband) wouldn't make such sudden movements because it triggers Duke's post-traumatic stress disorder. Faith said she was there to lend balance in the relationship—the perfect companion to do so because she, too, had been abused. She was teaching Duke to be patient and refined

Name: Grady

Breed: Golden Retriever

Grady was being walked with a younger Golden on the evening I encountered him. He lay down and allowed me to stroke him as he told me about his arthritis. He also felt pressure around his throat

(his owner confirmed that he seemed to have labored breathing; a vet appointment was pending). Grady understood he was passing the torch to the other dog as he was preparing to transition. But he wanted his owner to know he had a good life with her, and that he liked the little girl that came to visit (the owner said this was the young daughter of a friend). He also sensed the presence of an older female relative in spirit, who would waft through and check in on the family from time to time.

About four months later, I met up with Grady once again. His owner remembered me and, while she hadn't figured out who the older female relative was, she did say she had followed up with Grady's vet about his throat. To my surprise, the vet had told her that as Goldens age, their vocal chords constrict such that it creates pressure and decreased air flow, which causes a lot of panting. On this very cold day, however, Grady seemed just fine, I am happy to report.

Name: Phoebe
Breed: Saint Bernard

I'm just in from a walk on which I met Phoebe, a young (but large) Saint Bernard and her owner. Phoebe is as big as my aunt's dog, Orson, but not as husky. Once she calmed down a bit (awfully rambunctious at first, jumping up, etc.), she started talking. Her primary concern was that there was a man around her who raised his voice and yelled (the woman's son). It caused a lot of anxiety that settled in Phoebe's gut and caused her to have diarrhea (all true). The family also needed to know

that Phoebe gets into things she shouldn't, like getting up on countertops. The woman said Phoebe just ate an entire birthday cake that was left unattended on a counter top. Phoebe told me there's an older dog around her preparing to transition (true again!). She said her role was to be a protector for a baby who's coming. Her owner thought this pertained to the young dog her parents were getting, but I insisted it was an infant. As always, once I finished representing Phoebe's communication, she was very relaxed!

Name: Maggie
Breed: Australian Shepherd

I must preface discussing Maggie with two qualifications: a) She is my father's dog, and b) I have never liked her. My perception of Maggie has been that she is undisciplined and accustomed to being in control of her environment, for which she has been indulged in my opinion. I have taken to avoiding her, and the feeling's been mutual. So when my father asked me to talk with her, I declined the first couple times he made the request until one weekend afternoon when we were gathered in my aunt's sun porch. My father had again asked me to try communicating with her. This time I conceded with the caveat that I couldn't promise anything.

Maggie was resting under the table at our feet, and I sensed that she needed to pee, so I said so. My father disagreed and thought that if Maggie needed to go, she would get up and stand by the door. But at my aunt's chiding, he got up and took Maggie out. Guess what she did first thing out the door? Yup, she peed!

When they got back inside, Maggie started to open up. She said she's high-strung like my stepmother, but that it's in her heredity to be so. She likes everything

done in the same order and same sequence and kept predictable every day. She definitely does not like storms. She doesn't sleep well (a light sleeper) and doesn't like children. Her stomach feels queasy (which may be a side-effect of allergy medication). Most telling of all, Maggie was feeling conflicted about how to reconcile a worrisome scenario: She was anxious about something happening to my father on their daily walk on the mountain hillside behind their house—if he injured himself, should she stay and comfort him or should she go for help? (My stepmother jumped in at this point and confirmed that she and my father had been fussing about this very thing recently, and how my father won't carry a cell phone with him on his walks.) Maggie thinks the family cat lends balance to her hyper temperament. Once we got this all out, Maggie got calm and relaxed quite a bit. She even thanked me! Maybe there's hope for us yet.

Name: Shadow
Breed: Black Lab

I had seen Shadow on multiple occasions, but he always strained and pulled and barked at me and other walkers. On this particular day, I decided to try to introduce myself by kneeling down, being silent, and just letting him sniff my hand. He promptly bit it. Fortunately, I was wearing gloves! So much for Shadow.

Name: Unknown
Breed: Bulldog

I was approaching the dog with his owner while out for a walk. The owner was a portly man, who was on his cell phone during the entire interaction. As I knelt down to pet the dog (with the owner's permissive nod), I instantly got lots of very unpleasant, yucky feelings about the man; not that he was abusing the dog, just that he wasn't a very nice person. Not wanting to entertain this further, I pet the bulldog briefly and was on my way.

Name: Porter

Breed: Longhaired Poodle Mix

Porter is a very rambunctious one-year-old who is trying hard to control his chewing and would appreciate acknowledgement of such. He has great separation anxiety from Meg, his owner. She leaves one of her old sweatshirts with him, but I recommended something that makes a heartbeat sound. His anxiety settles in his stomach and gives him diarrhea, all true. He likes the taste of chicken. He also enjoys the little boy and girl that come to visit (Meg said that would be her nephew and niece). Porter also enjoys walking in the cool air and smelling the droppings of deer, raccoon, and other animal scents, all of which there are a lot of on our walking path.

Name: Max
Breed: Black Lab

Max greeted me enthusiastically at a holiday gathering in the home of a relative I've only previously visited once. Once things settled down, he opened up a bit. He was apologetic for having had an accident in the house in recent memory. When I asked the girlfriend of someone who lived there, she was unaware of anything. Max also indicated that his stomach was sensitive, and that he was afraid of storms, especially thunder. His role was to serve and protect. I revisited these points with the lady of the house who confirmed that when two of their cats are at odds, Max will insert himself (literally) as the equalizer between the two. She also said that three months ago, he had been overfed pasta by several visiting children and threw up in her bedroom. She said that even at the time, he seemed to really feel bad about it as he never has any kind of inside accident.

Name: Basco
Breed: Pomeranian

Basco spotted me approaching from afar and started a warning bark almost immediately. He then began racing toward me. As I stopped and squatted to greet him, he ran away and into his owner's arms. I spoke with him gently as his "mom" stroked him, though he seemed fearful and was trembling. I asked if Basco had always been with her, and she said he had. He began to calm a bit, and I had the impression that Basco was very nervous and anxious as a result of absorbing the depressive symptoms of his owner! As I was processing this, I observed the woman holding Basco more carefully and saw that she was rather unkempt-looking and her shoelaces were untied. This could be in keeping with what I was receiving from Basco. His irritable personality seemed to be a projection of his owner's symptoms of depression, which include loss of interest in personal hygiene and appearance.

Name: Lily

Breed: Boxer

Lily is an interesting anecdote because I never saw her, only her owner; but I was shown pictures of Lily. From those photos I was able to intuit some information about Lily long-distance. Lily is very young, but already very loyal to her new family. She is trying hard to control her chewing and is exerting effort to learn what's acceptable to chew and what is not. She is very curious about her surroundings and is inquisitive about another dog that she hears barking when outside. She also wonders about the horses that she smells and hears. Lily's owner confirmed that there are horses across the street from where they live. Lily is content and returns her owner's great affection for her.

Chapter Four

TEACHING US NEW TRICKS

Of my experiences conversing with dogs of varied breeds and backgrounds, I've come to a number of conclusions which I'd like to share here. As I've yet to meet *all* dogs, I am making generalizations and will qualify each entry by speculating that what I'm sharing applies to *most* dogs. Still, I think we can all benefit from appreciating the heightened sensitivities of our canine companions, and better understand them from an "inside-out" perspective. See if you concur.

1 **Most dogs understand their roles.** I've noticed an acceptance from dogs for their lot in life and their position in their respective households. even under

trying or unexpected conditions, such as introducing another animal, moving away, or welcoming a new baby, most dogs will make the best of it and adapt their role to the new circumstances, even taking the lead as nurturer and mentor of the new addition to the home. Some highly-strung dogs are not suitable to be around small children, but those with an even temperament readily accept the role of "mother," "guardian," or "protector," and enjoy the playful and entertaining energy young children exude. Most dogs perceive their role with duty and purpose, and they approach it in the same way you may view your own employment: You've got a job to do. Ever notice how dogs that are trained for certain jobs, such as service dogs or dogs that search for drugs or cadavers, really seem to conduct themselves with a sense of pride and responsibility when working? Your dog likely perceives himself similarly and desires the opportunity to fulfill his doggie mission.

2 **Most dogs understand the cycle of life.** The concept of life and death is a human-made one of finality founded on the belief that when we take our last breath, we cease existing as ourselves. But dogs appear to be all the wiser for knowing that our present forms are but a temporary façade. The dogs I've met who were older or preparing to transition

have all been absent of any concern or anxiety for what's coming next. They comprehend their purpose and know they will soon return to the source from which they originated (compare this with persons who have had near-death experiences and now say they no longer fear death). This is why we may agonize over the suffering of a dog in pain while they appear to accept it with extraordinary grace. This is not to suggest that we shouldn't do all we can to support our dogs' health, safety and welfare but know that dogs tend to face the inevitable with a greater understanding than some people.

3 Most dogs experience generation gaps.

Just like many human beings, there is a disparity between the canine generations such that, most often, younger or high-energy dogs are carefree, oblivious, and sometimes

quite daring and defiant (not unlike any number of teenagers). It is these dogs that I have found most difficult to communicate with when I've encountered them—they're so reckless or preoccupied, they just won't calm down long enough to focus! In my experience, older, more seasoned dogs have generally matured into their respective roles. In contrast with young dogs, the tone of an older dog's communication tends to be very deliberate, gracious and full

of civility. The older dogs are tolerant, patient or nurturing of the younger dogs but only to a point. Then they apply discipline in the form of nipping, snapping or other acts of dominance.

4 **Most dogs are empaths.**
I have gained a renewed appreciation for how deeply sensitive dogs can be; not just with respect to their supersonic hearing and sense of smell, but for their emotional capacity to react to the feelings of others. Many dogs worry about their owners and

other members of the household who are struggling with any number of stressors. In turn, those dogs may do their best to comfort humans with their humorous antics or by simply standing by with solidarity and complacence.

What people should be aware of is that, in my opinion, many dogs take on their owners' angst as their own; for being so emotionally sensitive, this can impact a dog psychologically and physically as the anxiety tends to settle in their gut and cause significant gastrointestinal upset. Suffice it to say, if your personality and home life is chaotic, this will be reflected in your dog's conduct. If your household is reasonably homeostatic and tranquil, your dog's personality is more likely to be reflective of this climate.

5 **Most dogs try to behave.**
I have met many dogs who "get" that they shouldn't be chewing things they've been directed away from or scolded about, but the urge can be irresistible. While some dogs communicate by deliberately misbehaving or defecating or urinating in plain

view, this is more a reflection of mistreatment or neglect by their owners. By and large, the dogs I have met understand what is expected of them and are making every effort to

comply with those expectations, such that when the occasional accident occurs (vomiting or incontinence), it is a shameful embarrassment for them and they are apologetic for their misstep. My little Cairn terrier had a very delicate stomach, but she understood that when she had to throw up, she should try to get to the vinyl flooring of the bathroom and avoid the carpet, which was sometimes more successful than others. On one occasion, I came home to discover that she had actually climbed into the bathtub, pooped neatly and jumped out when finished!

6 **Most small dogs are divas.**

I guess it's no wonder that most toy breeds mirror their ancestral heritage as descendants of lapdogs for the rich and famous. I have found most small dogs to have an aristocratic air of entitlement. They are not shy about asserting themselves. They can be fiercely loyal and affectionate, but on their terms. You will know readily whether you are "in" or "out." This has been my experience with many small dogs, as it takes them longer to make up their minds about whether I'm worthy of their time— or not, as the case may be. When they do open up, they are most likely to "dish" about their owners, to reiterate their position in the household and to air any cautions or complaints. (And for the record, I *like* small dogs. I have always  been partial to Pomeranians and terriers of all kinds.)

Most dogs want a little respect.

7 Just like people, dogs are possessed of gifts and talents and, as noted, accept and adapt to their respective roles within their owners' households. On a number of occasions, however, dogs have expressed to me their desire to be acknowledged and validated for what they do contribute. In other words, some owners become so distracted with life that they overlook, or take for granted, exactly how their dog benefits the family and fulfills their role in the household. If you suspect this to be true in your case, simply take time out to affirm to your dog that you appreciate all that she does, and that you recognize her good efforts. Don't be surprised if your expression of appreciation isn't reflected in your dog's conduct. In other words, the more you raise the bar in terms of outward recognition and acknowledgment for your dog's place as a family member, the more your dog is likely to meet those expectations.

8 **Most dogs want dog-time.** As human as they may seem at times, dogs just want to be dogs. This means they need regular, if not daily, time outdoors to walk, run, play and to take in all the exciting scents and tastes that motivate them to fully experience being a canine. Remember, dogs are descendants of wolves and require opportunities to interact with other dogs, to hunt or investigate, to problem solve and to apply gifts and talents particular to their breed, such as retrieving or protecting. As such, my "talking"

experiences while out on walks are probably an interruption for the dogs I've met! This is why typical dog behavior gets misinterpreted as *misbehavior*. Dogs cannot meet all of our expectations because they relapse into being what they are: Canines with canine instincts that can cause all but the most highly disciplined dogs to become overwhelmed and overcome with distraction. Forgive them these moments and rejoice in knowing that your dog loves being a dog.

9 Most dogs are intellectually diverse.
Also, like humans, dogs fall on a broad spectrum of intellect: from those seemingly dispossessed of much common sense to those who appear to spend a lot of time deep in thought. It makes me wonder, though, if the old adage "crazy like a fox" doesn't apply to those dogs who seem klutzy and comical. Is this a deliberate part of fulfilling their role to amuse and entertain as necessary? Some dogs may be more intellectually

Dogs cannot meet all of our
expectations because they
relapse into being what they are:
Canines with canine instincts

"advanced" in that they do a lot of careful observing and meditating, and prefer spending time in this way, rather than engaging with others. This seems especially true of older dogs that, due to physical limitations, may be compelled to refrain and reflect. As noted, it is not uncommon for a  younger, less worldly dog to be mentored by a mature or seasoned dog. This is precisely what occurred for two of my aunt's dogs once her dominant Golden Retriever, Morgan, passed away. The oldest remaining dog, Jonah, took the youngest dog, Orson, under her wing. This is remarkable in that she previously seemed to only tolerate him. She accepted the new challenge as nurturer, and, curiously, no longer nips at Orson when he goes outside; with Morgan gone, she can relax about anyone plotting to escape and can now enjoy herself outdoors.

10

Most dogs want to talk. With few exceptions, as you've read, there aren't many dogs who don't want to talk. Most are ready and want to know they're being listened to and acknowledged on this level. It has pleasantly surprised me to discover just how many dogs take advantage of the chance to communicate with me and immediately respond to my role as an interpreter in conveying information—sometimes pretty basic stuff—to their owners. The only limitations to knowing one's dog in

this manner are those imposed by the limit-makers. This may all be far-out-there stuff for some, I'll admit; hopefully the next chapter will break it down in a way that makes it accessible and conceivable to all.

Chapter Five

HOW IT WORKS

Learning how to talk to your dog telepathically may not be as farfetched as you think. In fact, most of you reading this are probably really ready without even realizing it. I'm going to do my best to spell it out in layperson's lingo, but some of this business of communicating with dogs may get a bit spiritual; for me, personally, I don't know how to present it any other way. So if you're a spiritually-minded person, think Saint Francis, patron saint of animals and proficient communicator of such. And if you're not spiritually-minded, think Dr. Doolittle, and it'll all be good.

Have you ever thought of a loved one and, a minute later, they text, e-mail or call you? Have you ever spontaneously laughed or cried together with a close friend? Or, as a parent, have you ever just *known* that your child needed you and, in that moment, it turns out they really did? Like most of us, you can probably relate to those times when you are intuitively connected with people who are important or dear to you. This isn't about being psychic; it's about the emotional nature of the relationship you share with those individuals.

The preceding examples are times when our hearts and minds align not only within ourselves but with our loved ones, so that we are connected naturally and without words. If you pause to list why you love and adore people dear to you, pay attention to the *emotions* you feel that correlate to the traits and attributes you list. You may even choose to call up specific memories of those occasions when you really connected with someone. If you reflect on the emotion of those memories, you'll find it was a positive, joyful, loving or purposeful feeling that bonded you with them.

Now, think about your dog in the same manner. Pay attention to the thoughts, sensations and emotions that may come to mind as you reflect on your dog, and all the reasons why he tries your patience, gives love freely, or knows just how to comfort you in the right moment. How did you receive the information? Was it in terms of an emotional response in your heart that felt warm or made you tear up? Did the feelings come in the form of images or impressions that recalled specific incidents or milestones you shared with your dog? It will be important to note this. This emotional

connection, and the feeling it gives you, is the vehicle that will support your ability to talk to your dog.

What most people don't know about me, until now, is that I've been working part-time as a professional psychic-clairvoyant since 2004. What I discovered was that my ability to intuitively connect to children, teens and adults with autism, and to translate their intentions authentically (as opposed to what gets misinterpreted as bad behavior), could extend to include *anyone*. If you remember the Magic 8-Ball, you'll appreciate how it works for me. The Magic 8-Ball was a popular novelty of the late 1960s. It was shaped like an oversized black pool table 8-ball filled with an inky black liquid. On the base of the Magic 8-Ball was a small, clear window. The idea was that the Magic 8-Ball was a mystical prophet and could respond to any inquiry made of it by the user making a request, shaking the ball, turning it over to see the little window, and waiting a second or two for the written answer to float to the surface of the window (I usually got "Ask again later").

This concept is sort of like what happens in my head and what I'd like to see happen for you. When I focus on my client, I get pictures, movies and impressions specific to that person. For example, in a session with one client, I was puzzled about seeing Mary Poppins singing about a spoonful of sugar helping to swallow medicine. When I asked my client what it meant, she explained that her deceased mother was named

Mary, and a childhood memory was of Mary chasing her through the house trying to get my client to take her spoonful of medicine!

Sometimes I'll see a word, or words, paired with an image, like when a client was asking about potentially relocating for employment, and I saw the word "Tennessee." Turns out she had connections there and moving to Tennessee was not beyond the realm of probability.

What people fail to realize about psychics is that, like the Magic 8-Ball, the imagery received is rarely crystal-clear, or it may take a moment to surface through the haze in order to make sense or be interpreted.

Clairvoyance, or clear-seeing, is usually how I receive information. Sometimes I'll get a feeling or just know what to say; this is called clairsentience. Others may receive information that corresponds with the senses of hearing, smelling, or tasting. However, the neat thing about being human is that receiving intuitive information may look differently in you than it does in me—we're uniquely created individuals and no two of us are alike!

Now, re-think my earlier request for remembering a loved one. On revisiting the concept of being attentive to the visceral reaction you feel associated with that person, are you "getting" anything visual, emotional or auditory, or even a smell or taste you might link in memory with that individual? For example, does thinking about a beloved grandma recall her perfume or the cinnamon scent of her homemade

pastries? Does remembering your favorite uncle bring to mind images of him swinging a golf club or his love of anchovies? These are the kinds of impressions you'll want to carefully note.

Next, try doing the same thing but, instead, think about your dog. Does the doggie scent of his fur seem almost real as you recollect the last time he got wet? Can you "see" the day he played catch in the park? Try to call-up as much detail as possible while you're "in the zone" of remembering. If it's not working for you just yet, or if you're feeling stuck, don't get too frustrated. This is a *process* that can take significant time to develop, and it may come more easily to some than to others.

For instance, as a person on the autism spectrum, I *naturally* possess heightened sensitivities *and* I think in pictures and movies, that is, constant streams of visual imagery. If you say "dog" to me, I immediately start flipping through my mental Rolodex of images related to that word. I might see the last dog I met; I might see the dog breeds chart on my vet's wall; I might conjure the image of a snapshot of me with a dog; or I might see dogs with whom I've had various relationships over the years. It's sort of a visual form of word-association. You may very well not think this way, but you *can* do it if someone directs you to by saying, "Picture this…" or "Imagine this…" It just may require greater effort on your part.

Another interesting autism parallel to share with you is that Temple Grandin, perhaps the world's best-known person with autism, contends in her book, *Animals in Translation*, that living creatures think primarily in terms of imagery. I'll take that a step further and suggest that living creatures think in terms of imagery *and* emotional response. I recently watched a very moving video of a young elephant calf mourning the death of its mother. It was nearly unbearable to see the calf draping its trunk over the prostrate corpse of the deceased elephant with such reverence that the emotion was almost palpable.

In each of my three books that connect autism and spirituality, there are anecdotes about the propensity of some individuals with autism to interact with, interpret and understand animals. This kind of relationship, and the level of understanding that comes with it, occurs naturally for some with autism. I intend absolutely no disrespect when I say that this is plausible because many individuals with autism share similar traits with animals. What I mean by this is that not only do many people with autism think in pictures, they may also possess the purity of acute senses and uncorrupted emotions in the very primitive and authentic way that animals do. I am *not* suggesting that autistics are like animals in terms of behavior, and anyone who is familiar with my work knows that I am a staunch advocate for respecting the intellect of people with autism. I am referring, here, to heightened sensitivities that make the swapping of imagery and emotion ("communicating" if you will) between humans and animals a very facile and natural process. Children and highly sensitive people can often share similarly-attuned experiences. Some people with autism also share another commonality with dogs that you will want to emulate: They don't speak and, therefore, they live in silence.

So, if you're serious about talking to dogs, I encourage you to become more like them! No, this doesn't mean getting down on all fours, sniffing and barking. It means consciously devoting energy to developing your intuitive gifts and spending time in silence. You'll get back whatever you put into it, which means that if you don't invest much time or thought into the process, you can expect little in return.

However, if you desire to become more open and aware to the possibility of connecting with dogs in this manner, and you devote time to doing so, your chances of being successful are much greater.

If you are of a religious or spiritual persuasion, you can open yourself up through silent prayer. Spending solitary time absorbed in prayer is an excellent way of setting your intentions and allowing yourself the opportunity to understand how you, and what you contribute, fit into the grand scheme of the universe. It is also a time to express appreciation for your many blessings in life and to acknowledge a higher power as the source. During these moments, you can request aid and support in developing a means of better communicating with dogs through silent interaction with them, such as image-swapping. Spending time in prayer with the intention of enhancing your spiritual gifts and talents will be most effective if you set aside time for it *every day*, even if it's only for a few minutes.

If you are neither religious nor spiritual, you can achieve the same, or similar, effect by meditating to a guided imagery CD. There are many available from which to select, and you may wish to sample one or two before deciding upon one that "feels" comfortable enough for you to use it often, if not daily. Many such recordings take the listener on an auditory journey. Most have spiritual undertones by expressing unity and oneness and clarifying personal introspection. One thing that they all have in common is to set the stage for you to cultivate your imagination through visualizing that which is being described, and further personalizing your visions as uniquely your own. We should never fear our imagination! After all, the chair in which you are now seated originated in someone's imagination.

If prayer or meditation is not a consideration because of time constraints, the most natural way of engaging this process is to simply build upon something that most pet owners already do on a daily basis: Walk the dog. Walking the dog = meditation time. Now, I have seen many dog walkers who use the opportunity to talk on the cell phone, listen to their iPods or chat with the person who accompanies them. This is not mediation time. Remember, you want to spend time in silence, just like your dog does. So, while you're walking the dog (*alone*) make

the most of the chance to assimilate all you survey around you; encourage yourself to find at least one thing of beauty to admire, and appreciatively drink in any sights, scents and sounds offered by the outdoors. Do this *every day*. (And if you don't walk your dog, at least spend time quietly in the same space as they do, preferably outside.) The purpose in doing this is to awaken your consciousness and get you thinking and responding to your environment more like a dog does.

An aftereffect of investing time in practicing prayer, meditation or silent reflection, is that you can begin to pay greater attention to the impressions you receive that may seem intuitive. Are you getting any visuals in your mind's eye? Are they relevant to your dog? What about any emotions or feelings? Earlier, I wrote of the special alignment between hearts and minds—are you sensing this when you are in solitude with your dog? Have you tried imagining what it would be like to be your dog, to take his or her position and to suggest what he or she might be taking in pertaining to their surroundings? These are all areas to which you may begin to expand your thinking by giving over some deep thought and consideration.

As you are growing and learning, bear in mind the importance of proper validation. If you can't authenticate what you supposed to be communication from a dog, then it is only speculation until proven otherwise. Proper validation can come directly from a dog's owner (if that's not you) or from observing the dog's behavior to see if he or she does what they "said" they would. I also think it's a good thing to be skeptical, and to attempt to reconcile a rational solution to an occurrence that appears out of the ordinary on the surface. Remember: *Not everything is something*, such as the case when a dog's owner said to me, "He really likes you!" because her dog was licking my chin when, in fact, I knew what the dog *really* liked was the smell of my flavored

Chapstick! My advice, then, is to approach talking to dogs with childlike wonder and optimism for unconventional possibilities; but do stay grounded and don't go overboard to the point of making others think you're slightly cuckoo. In other words, keep it real and maintain a balanced perspective!

Chapter Six:

Good Doggie

In this final chapter of *Conversations with Dogs*, I am providing you with some exercises for stretching your consciousness and strengthening your relationships with dogs. Here's where the rubber meets the road, and you can now begin putting into real-time practice some suggested concepts for connecting with dogs. You may be in the best frame of mind to attempt these exercises if you've first spent time in silent contemplation and then identified the manner in which you receive intuitive information such as sights, sounds, feelings and so on.

If at first you are not successful, don't be discouraged. This process of communicating without words can take time. Think of it like learning a foreign language—you didn't become fluent (if ever!) after only the first few lessons of French or Spanish; it required practice to formulate the most rudimentary of reciprocal interactions.

Give yourself time and know, too, that the dog, or dogs, you've chosen to focus on may not be as open to letting you in as much as you want to be let in. In other words, this is a trust issue. If you've been as loyal and loving to your pet as he's been to you, it will likely be an experience that is simply a natural extension of the terrific relationship you've already established. If you have only ever seen your dog as just that, a dog, it could take more time. But it all depends on you, your attitude and your approach. Curiously, what I have found occurs most often after dogs communicate with me is that they tend to become very affectionate and appreciative (it's an intimate process, this business of connecting intuitively). They also tend to become quite relaxed and calm. See if this holds true in your experiences as well. You may also wish to keep a written journal to document your progress. A year from now, you might just be surprised at how your diligence has prospered into something extraordinary.

Exercise 1: Sending

For this exercise, go into a space separate from your dog, and try simply calling your dog to you by name, but *only* in your mind. Focus not only on your dog's name but think about how you decided upon that particular name, why you decided it suited her best, and how she learned to equate the name as synonymous with her being.

Exercise 2: Sending

This exercise builds on the preceding name-calling experiment, but instead of calling your dog's name, try "sending" specific visualizations, like picturing your dog's favorite treat. Don't just picture the treat, but think about it like your dog does: Smells and tastes. Try conjuring in your mind a combination of the image of the treat, you giving the treat to your dog and how it likely tastes and smells to your dog. (And make certain you've got some handy for when your dog responds by coming to you, tail wagging in anticipation, from the other room!)

Exercise 3: Sending

Implement exercise #3 as you did #2, but this time "send" the word and sensory sensations associated with *walk*. I'm also asking you to try this exercise at a time of day that is *not* your dog's usual time for a walk. This is a test of validation, especially if your dog brings you his leash! Remember to include with the thought "walk" what your dog associates with that activity such as sounds, scents, visuals, and so on.

Exercise 4: Sending

For this exercise, be present in the same room with your dog. Try focusing on a specific emotion that you link to your dog, like humor, love or gratitude. As you do this, silently recall events you've shared with your dog that exemplify that emotion, like the first time your dog saw you and kissed your face; or the time he made a mess, but you laughed instead of scolded; or the appreciation you feel for how protective your dog is of your children or other pets. Allow yourself time to register in your heart the emotion the memory creates. During this process, monitor your dog's reaction and see if he reacts in kind, such as by moving closer to you, laying his head in your lap or showing affection through other means.

Exercise 5: Receiving

This time, we're going to change things up a bit and practice waiting for imagery to come from your dog. Practice doing this by first starting out simply. With your dog nearby, silently and in your mind send her a visual choice between two things, such as two snacks or two favored activities, in the manner described in the preceding exercises. Remain still and calm, and wait to see if you receive intuitive impressions that indicate a preference for one or the other, such as sights, sounds, feelings or scents. Once you feel your dog has communicated a choice, follow through by acting on it and delivering the selected option.

Exercise 6: Receiving

Building upon exercise #5, similarly, try silently sending your dog a question such as "How do you feel (physically)?" or "Do you have any concerns you wish to share?" When doing this, focus on the emotion you are conveying, not just the words; it is the intention of the communication that matters most. Pay attention to any impressions you may receive in reciprocation. *It is unlikely that your dog will reply in a way that is like a spoken voice carrying on a conversation with you.* You are most apt to receive emotions, feelings, visuals and so on. For example, when my aunt requested that I ask her dying Golden Retriever about the status of his health, I "felt" some pressure around my throat (in the region corresponding to his tumors), and I "saw" him showing me a setting sun. These impressions are symbolisms that I, as the doggie interpreter, then translated into language.

As you've read, these exercises aren't rocket science; in fact, they are actually very simple. Sometimes the so-called "powers" possessed by others have been sensationalized, glamorized or complicated to the point that the layperson has been led to believe such attributes are outside the grasp of the average Joe. Not so! We *all* hold the capacity to tap the intuitive or spiritual aspect of our personality—it is not reserved for a select few. Please stay the course, hold high your positive beliefs, and practice over a period of time to hone your skills.

A word of caution: If you decide to begin applying your new talent to dogs other than your own, please exercise discretion. Unless you don't mind people perceiving you as a bit nutty, take care about when, where and with whom you reveal that you communicate with dogs. Not everyone is open to hearing about it and some will be entirely dismissive. Keep in mind that this falls into the category of psychic stuff for many people, and that may present personal, ethical or religious conflict for disbelievers.

Case in point: I was waiting for my car during an oil change, and a

man in the sitting area had two dogs with him who seemed friendly enough: Rob, a black Pit Bull, and Ava, an Irish Setter. Ava was especially outgoing, so I took the liberty of divulging to the man that I could talk to dogs, that I think in pictures like dogs do, that we exchange images, and that I was writing a book all about it.

(Talk about overkill!) In so doing, I breached some social protocols which I chalk up to my autistic tendencies, but there's a lesson to be learned here for all. Not only were we in a public place with other people within earshot, I put the man in a rather awkward position. He did say that he wanted to hear what Ava had to tell me, and Ava shared how sensitive she is, and how she's patient with Rob when he gets into things or lacks good manners. But when I got one thing that didn't jive for the owner (Ava thought her owner drives too fast), he seemed to tune out. This made for a very awkward situation. When the man got up to leave, he didn't acknowledge me or say goodbye, and I can only imagine the impression I left on him.

In light of this anecdote, I would advise that it's best to fine-tune your skills with trusted allies first—such as dog owners who are friends—to develop a reasonable degree of accuracy before venturing to apply those skills to dogs with whom you are unfamiliar.

Unless and until you feel like you're ready to start talking to unfamiliar dogs, it may be advisable to invest some practice time in careful observation of any number of dogs to see if what you suspect they are communicating with you is actually authentic. For example, if you are watching a dog being walked or sitting next to its owner, try connecting with that dog silently in the same way that you've learned to do with your own dog. You might try sending the impression of emotions, such as happiness and love, or you may send images associated with peacefulness. See if the dog reacts, makes eye contact or acknowledges you in any way.

If you decide to approach a strange dog for the purpose of communicating, it's proper form to ask permission of the owner first before talking to the dog, just as you should before you pet any unfamiliar animal. Ask yourself too, is this an appropriate time and place? Am I interrupting or intruding, or does the dog owner seem receptive to chatting about their dog? Are others nearby? Is it okay to open up and speak frankly? If you develop a chatty rapport with a dog owner first, and their dog seems drawn to you, you might broach the subject by saying: "Your dog seems to have a lot he wants to say. I'm pretty good at interpreting dog behavior. Would you like to know what I think he's telling us?" or some such similar banter that is benign, up for interpretation and not overly intrusive. If a dog is indicating that he loves playing with a child in the household, you might say something rather generic along the lines of: "Your dog seems like he'd be good with kids." Then gauge whether to continue based on the owner's reaction.

The process of better understanding dogs starts with better understanding ourselves. Remember, we all have gifts and talents, and we all hold the capacity to communicate on any number of levels including without words, just like our canine companions. You may also find that enhancing your sensitivity for dogs may positively enhance the way you interact with friends, family and co-workers. You may develop a renewed patience and compassion for others as well, in the way that most dogs tend to be welcoming, affectionate, and unconditional in their devotion. Dogs don't think in terms of discrimination and prejudice, nor do they differentiate between who is attractive, physically disabled, or emotionally capable. They give their love and comfort to whomever is willing to receive it, oftentimes intuitively. If we could all learn to conduct ourselves more like dogs do, we might learn more about how to get along better with one another. And that wouldn't be a bad thing at all.

The process of better understanding dogs

starts with better understanding ourselves.

About the Author

William Stillman is the award-winning author of special needs parenting books including *Autism and the God Connection*, *The Soul of Autism*, and *The Autism Prophecies*, a trilogy that correlates aspects of autism with metaphysical themes. Stillman's work has resonated with parents, professionals and persons with autism internationally, and has received endorsements of praise from bestselling authors and spiritual pioneers Gary Zukav, Carol Bowman, Dean Hamer and Larry Dossey. To date, his books have been translated in four languages.

Stillman's spiritual work led to him contributing a week of daily reflections for the 2009 edition of *Disciplines: A Book of*

Daily Devotions and creating a training module for The Thoughtful Christian, a Web-based resource organization. Since 2006, Stillman has been a regular guest on BeyondtheOrdinary.net, an online radio program devoted to uncommon topics. He has also been interviewed on numerous radio shows of a paranormal nature including *Coast to Coast A.M.*, the most listened to overnight program in North America. Stillman has taught a course on developing intuition and has twice presented for Lily Dale Assembly, the country's oldest spiritualist community. Since 2004, Stillman has worked professionally as a psychic-clairvoyant for Alta View Wellness Center in Harrisburg, Pennsylvania.

ABOUT THE PUBLISHER

Haunted Road Media

Haunted Road Media, LLC
Explore With Us

Haunted Road Media, LLC is a multimedia publishing and production company that specializes in the paranormal, mysterious events, and historic curiosities. Our primary focus is on the publishing industry and video production promoting the talents of artists, authors, and musicians alike.

More information about Haunted Road Media may be found at:

www.hauntedroadmedia.com